Instant Highcharts

Learn to create dynamic and customized charts instantly using Highcharts

Cyril Grandjean

PUBLISHING

BIRMINGHAM - MUMBAI

Instant Highcharts

Copyright © 2013 Packt Publishing

First published: July 2013

Production Reference: 1220713

Published by Packt Publishing Ltd.
Livery Place
35 Livery Street
Birmingham B3 2PB, UK.

ISBN 978-1-84969-754-5

www.packtpub.com

Credits

Author

Cyril Grandjean

Reviewers

Stéphanie DREVET

Rémi LEPAGE

Acquisition Editor

Martin Bell

Commissioning Editor

Amit Ghodake

Technical Editor

Shashank Desai

Project Coordinator

Esha Thakker

Proofreader

Aaron Nash

Production Coordinator

Melwyn D'sa

Cover Work

Melwyn D'sa

Cover Image

Valentina Dsilva

About the Author

Cyril Grandjean is graduated from the school Supinfo (France) and from Oxford Brookes University (United Kingdom). He is currently working for company Ausy as a software engineer. During his professional experience, he has mainly developed web projects in PHP or Java. He also spends some of his spare time developing applications in C# or mobile applications. On his website `www.cyril-grandjean.co.uk`, he also writes some articles about software development. During his past job for the company Distrame, he contributed to the development of a solution called Efficacenergie, which measures the energy consumption (electricity, water, gas, and so on) of a building. By accessing a web interface developed with Ext-JS library, customers can analyze their own energy consumption through customizable charts developed with Highcharts library.

About the Reviewers

Stéphanie DREVET is an engineer, born in 1980 in France.

She did her scientific studies in Lyon (MPSI*) and completed her graduation from the Engineering school Ecole des Mines de Nancy.

She has been working on computer science projects for Airline IT since 2003, on the French Riviera.

She is passionate about web technologies and artistic creations. To combine both, she created her website http://www.prettypix.fr in 2012, where she exhibits her artistic work.

Rémi LEPAGE is a freelance software engineer and a computer science technical trainer.

He holds a master's degree in Computer Science from Supinfo and the ZCE (Zend Certified Engineer) PHP 5.3 certification.

Specialized in web application development and database administration, he created several management intranets. He is currently creating enterprise applications.

www.packtpub.com

Support files, eBooks, discount offers and more

You might want to visit www.packtpub.com for support files and downloads related to your book.

Did you know that Packt offers eBook versions of every book published, with PDF and ePub files available? You can upgrade to the eBook version at www.packtpub.com and as a print book customer, you are entitled to a discount on the eBook copy. Get in touch with us at service@packtpub.com for more details.

At www.packtpub.com, you can also read a collection of free technical articles, sign up for a range of free newsletters and receive exclusive discounts and offers on Packt books and eBooks.

packtlib.packtpub.com

Do you need instant solutions to your IT questions? PacktLib is Packt's online digital book library. Here, you can access, read and search across Packt's entire library of books.

Why Subscribe?

- ✦ Fully searchable across every book published by Packt
- ✦ Copy and paste, print and bookmark content
- ✦ On demand and accessible via web browser

Free Access for Packt account holders

If you have an account with Packt at www.packtpub.com, you can use this to access PacktLib today and view nine entirely free books. Simply use your login credentials for immediate access.

Table of Contents

Instant Highcharts

Welcome to *Instant Highcharts*. This book has been especially created to provide you with all the information that you need to get set up with Highcharts. You will learn the basics of Highcharts, get started with building your first charts, and discover some tips and tricks for using Highcharts.

This book contains the following sections:

So what is Highcharts? finds out what Highcharts actually is, what you can do with it, and why it's so great.

Installation enables you to learn how to download and install Highcharts with a minimum fuss, and then set it up so that you can use it as soon as possible.

Quick start – setting up main sections of Highcharts gives you an overview of how to perform one of the core tasks of Highcharts: creating charts. Follow the steps to create your own chart, which will be the basis of most of your work with Highcharts.

Top 4 features you need to know about will help you in learning how to perform the four tasks with the most important features of Highcharts. By the end of this section you will be able to create a line chart with a time axis and two Y-axes, a stacked column chart, a pie chart, and create dynamic charts with your own data.

People and places you should get to know will inform you about the people associated with this book. Every open source project is centered on a community. This section provides you with many useful links to the project page and forums, as well as a number of helpful articles, tutorials, blogs, and the Twitter feeds of Highcharts super-contributors.

So, what is Highcharts?

Highcharts is a JavaScript library that will allow you to implement interactive and dynamic charts inside your web application. Highcharts has been written in pure HTML5 and JavaScript, which will allow you to display charts made with Highcharts natively in your web browser without using any plugins such as Adobe Flash or Microsoft Silverlight. Another strength of Highcharts is that Highcharts' charts are created with SVG or VML (for Internet Explorer), which are vector image formats. Compared to the image format that are using pixels, such as JPEG, PNG or GIF, the vector image formats doesn't lose quality if the image is displayed bigger. Therefore, with Highcharts, you will be able to display your charts on any size of screen without any difference in terms of chart quality. Nevertheless, it is possible to export your chart in JPEG, PNG, or GIF by using the export module.

With Version 3.0 of Highcharts, you can create a large variety of charts including not only line, column, bar, pie charts, but also angular gauges and polar charts. The main benefit of Highcharts is the ability to combine different charts, and also the possibility of customization. With Highcharts, there are a lot of possibilities, such as adding multiple axes, customizing the tool tip according to your data, adding several plot bands and plot lines to your graph, and changing the legend position.

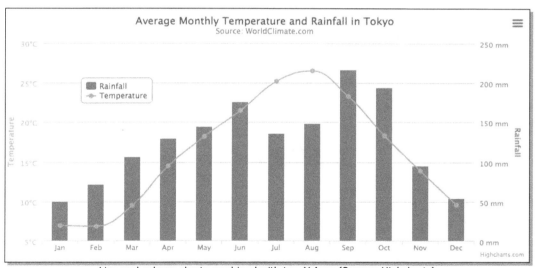

Line and column charts combined with two Y-Axes (Source: Highcharts)

With Highcharts, you can implement some interactive features, such as the ability to zoom into some parts of your chart (for example, refer to the following chart), add a point to your chart dynamically, and refresh the data at runtime.

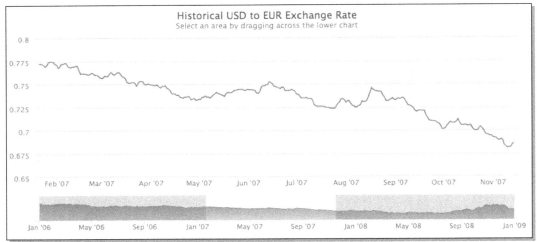

Zoom inside some parts of the chart (Source: Highcharts)

Finally, with Highcharts, it is also possible to draw your own shape inside your web application. This feature will allow you to create your own chart, if the large variety of charts already provided by Highcharts doesn't answer your needs.

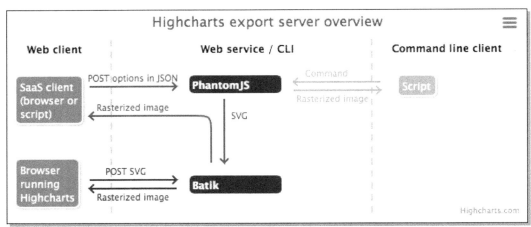

Customized drawing with Highcharts (Source: Highcharts)

Installation

In four easy steps, you can install Highcharts and get it set up on your web application.

Step 1 – what do I need?

Before you install Highcharts, you will need to check that you have all of the required elements, as shown in the following list:

✦ **Web browser**: In order to work properly, you need to use at least the following versions or higher of these web browsers, Internet Explorer 6, Firefox 2, Chrome 1, Safari 4, Opera 9, iOS 3.0, Android 2 (Limited support).

✦ **IDE** or **Text Editor**: You can use any text editor or **Integrated Development Environment** (**IDE**) in order to create your Highcharts charts, but it is recommended to have syntax highlighting for JavaScript. You can use Notepad++ for Windows or Fraise on Mac OS X, which are good free tools that include this feature.

✦ **JavaScript framework**: It is recommended to use at least one the following versions or higher; jQuery 1.3, Mootools 1.2, Prototype 1.7, Ext-JS 3.

Step 2 – downloading Highcharts

The easiest way to download Highcharts is in a compressed package from the website at http://www.highcharts.com/download.

Download the most current stable build. The Version 3.0.2 of Highcharts has been used in book samples. After downloading and unpacking the archive, you will be left with a directory called Highcharts with the version number, containing a number of files and folders.

In the js directory, you will find two versions of Highcharts library, highcharts.js and highcharts.src.js. highcharts.js (131 Ko) is the minified version of highcharts. src.js (416 Ko).

 Because the minified version is lighter, it is recommended to use this version when your application is deployed in production in order to improve the performances of your application. The non-minified version can be used during the development phase.

Step 3 – Highcharts installation

In order to use Highcharts, you need to include your Highcharts code in the head section of your HTML. You can put your JavaScript code directly into your web server, and use the path of your JavaScript files or include the code using an external URL. For each of the JavaScript frameworks, we will show you how to integrate Highcharts inside your application by using an external URL. For Mootools and Prototype libraries, an adapter script has to be included as well in order to work properly.

✦ jQuery framework

```
<script src="http://ajax.googleapis.com/ajax/libs/jquery/1.8.2/
jquery.min.js"></script>
<script src="http://code.highcharts.com/highcharts.js"></script>
```

✦ Mootools framework

```
<script src="https://ajax.googleapis.com/ajax/libs/mootools/1.4.5/
mootools-yui-compressed.js"></script>
<script src="http://code.highcharts.com/adapters/mootools-adapter.
js"></script>
<script src="http://code.highcharts.com/highcharts.js"></script>
```

✦ Prototype framework

```
<script src="https://ajax.googleapis.com/ajax/libs/prototype/1.7/
prototype.js"></script>
<script src="http://code.highcharts.com/adapters/prototype-
   adapter.js"></script>
<script src="http://code.highcharts.com/highcharts.js"></script>
```

 If you want to follow JavaScript best practices, and improve the performances of your application in production, you can minify your own code into one JavaScript file, and include the JavaScript files before the end of the body section of your HTML.

If you want to use the optional export module, you will also need to include the following code inside the head section of your HTML.

```
<script src="http://code.highcharts.com/modules/exporting.js"></
script>
```

If you want to render your printable images on your own web server, please follow the instructions available at `http://www.highcharts.com/component/content/article/2-news/52-serverside-generated-chart`.

Step 4 – your first chart

Now that you have imported Highcharts into your web application, we will create our first chart. Nevertheless, before creating any JavaScript code, you will have to create an HTML div element identified by a chosen HTML ID with a defined size.

```
<div id="myFirstChartContainer" style="width:600px; height:400px;"></
div>
```

Then, you can create your chart in JavaScript inside the script element in the head section of your HTML. You need to include your own code after the inclusion of your framework and Highchart library as indicated in the previous step. For each of the previous frameworks, we will show you how to create your first chart.

+ jQuery framework

```
$(function () {
    var chart = new Highcharts.Chart({({
        chart: {
            type: 'column'
        },
        title: {
            text: 'Sales by city'
        },
        xAxis: {
            categories: ['London', 'Paris', 'Madrid']
        },
        yAxis: {
            title: {
                text: 'Sales'
            }
        },
        series: [{
            name: 'Cities',
            data: [1000, 2500, 1500]
        }]
    });
});
```

+ Mootools framework

```
window.addEvent('domready', function() {
    var chart = new Highcharts.Chart({
        chart: {
            renderTo: 'myFirstChartContainer',
            type: 'column'
        },
        title: {
```

```
                    text: 'Sales by city'
            },
            xAxis: {
                categories: ['London', 'Paris', 'Madrid']
            },
            yAxis: {
                title: {
                    text: 'Sales'
                }
            },
            series: [{
                name: 'Cities',
                data: [1000, 2500, 1500]
            }]
        });
    });
```

✦ Prototype framework

```
document.observe("dom:loaded", function() {
    var chart = new Highcharts.Chart({
        chart: {
            renderTo: 'myFirstChartContainer',
            type: 'column'
        },
        title: {
            text: 'Sales by city'
        },
        xAxis: {
            categories: ['London', 'Paris', 'Madrid']
        },
        yAxis: {
            title: {
                text: 'Sales'
            }
        },
        series: [{
            name: 'Cities',
            data: [1000, 2500, 1500]
        }]
    });
});
```

Downloading the example code

You can download the example code files for all Packt books you have purchased from your account at `http://www.packtpub.com`. If you purchased this book elsewhere, you can visit `http://www.packtpub.com/support` and register to have the files e-mailed directly to you.

Each of the JavaScript frameworks has its own constructor, and their own way to link to div element. For jQuery, the div ID will be included directly in the constructor, but you will have to use the `renderTo` element for Prototype and Mootools. Nevertheless, the code inside the constructor will be the same whatever framework you use. The code in the following sections will use jQuery, but you can easily reuse the code with other JavaScript frameworks.

And that's it

By this point, you should have your Highcharts working, free to play around and discover more about it.

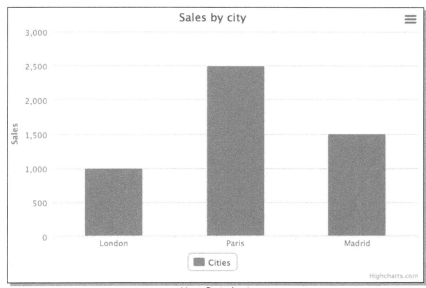

Your first chart

Quick start – setting up the main sections of Highcharts

A Highcharts' chart is composed of several parts, which could be mandatory or optional parts depending on the chart that you will create. In this section, we will show you the main elements that are composing a Highcharts' chart, and we will reuse the chart, previously created in order to illustrate these different core concepts.

Step 1 – setting the title and subtitle

For each Highcharts' chart, you can set a title and a subtitle. In the previous section, we have already declared the chart with the title **Sales by city**. We will now add a subtitle section with the text **Statistics of 2012**.

1. Add the subtitle section and set the text to **Statistics of 2012**:

    ```
    subtitle: {
        text: 'Statistics of 2012'
    }
    ```

2. You should have the expected result as shown in the following chart:

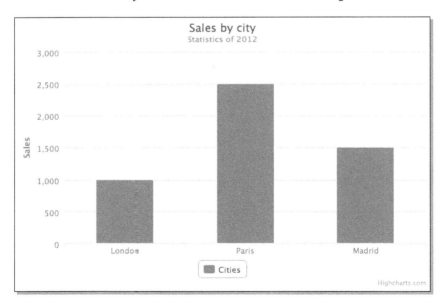

Step 2 – setting the credits

In the credits parts, you will be able to set the source or the copyright of your chart. By default, it is set to **Highcharts.com**. We will change this default value to **Packt Publishing**. The URL of the credit by default is `http://www.highcharts.com`, but you can change it by setting the `href` parameter with your own URL. We will change this value with `http://www.packtpub.com`.

1. Add the credit section and set the text to `Packt Publishing` and set the `href` section with `http://www.packtpub.com`:

```
credits: {
    text: 'Packt Publishing',
    href: 'http://www.packtpub.com'
}
```

2. You should have the expected result as shown in the following chart:

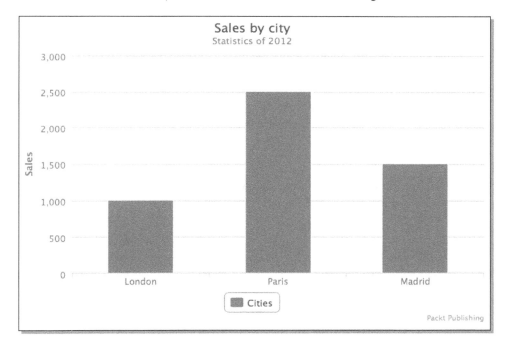

Step 3 – setting the series

The series section is a mandatory one of Highcharts, which you will have to include for every chart, that you will create. A series is simply a set of data that will be defined with a name and an array of data. We will now modify the previous series section by adding another section that will represent the sales of two different years for the three cities already defined:

1. Rename the previous `series` with the name `2011` and add another `series` with the name `2012` and a new set of data:

```
series: [{
      name: '2011',
      data: [1000, 2500, 1500]
   },
   {
      name: '2012',
      data: [1200, 2200, 1700]
}]
```

2. You should have the expected result as shown in the following chart:

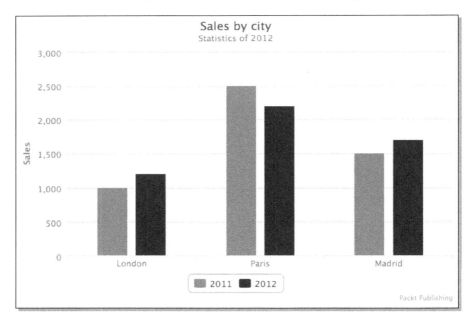

Step 4 – setting the axes, plot lines, and plot bands

The axes sections will be set for some charts, such as line and column charts, but will not be included for charts, such as pie charts or donut charts. Axes are divided into two types: Y Axes and X Axes. Then, each axis is divided into four categories:

✦ **Linear Axis**: This category of axis will use a linear scale like our Y Axis.

✦ **Logarithmic Axis**: This category of axis will follow a logarithmic scale.

✦ **Category Axis**: This axis will display different categories of data. Our X-Axis is a category axis.

✦ **Time Axis**: You will have to use this category of axis when you want to represent your data along a time axis.

By default, the axis is calculated automatically, but you can set a minimum or maximum value if you set the 'min' and 'max' parameters of your axis. Then, you can add plot lines and plot bands for each of your axes. Plot lines and plot bands can be used when you want to display a limit or when you want to point out some parts of your axis.

For our chart, we will add a plot line, which will represent the best sales of the company and a plot band, which will represent the expected sales:

1. For the plot line, we add our element inside the `plotLines` section of our Y Axis with a red color set in hexadecimal format with a width of 2 pixels and a value set to 2500.

```
plotLines: [{
    color: '#FF0000',
    width: 2,
    value: 2500
}]
```

2. Then, for the plot band, we add our element inside the `plotBands` section of our Y Axis with a green color set in RGBA format from the values 1000 to 1500. The fourth parameter of our `rgba` function will allow us to have a bit of transparency. This parameter has to be set between zero (Transparent) and one (Opaque). We will also add a label with a text set to `Expected Sales`.

```
plotBands: [{
    color: 'rgba(124,252,0, 0.3)',
    from: 1000,
    to: 1500,
    label: {
        text: 'Expected Sales'
    }
}]
```

3. For your `yAxis`, you should have the following code:

```
yAxis: {
   title: {
      text: 'Sales'
   },
   plotLines: [{
      color: '#FF0000',
      width: 2,
      value: 2500
   }],
   plotBands: [{
      color: 'rgba(124,252,0, 0.3)',
      from: 1000,
      to: 1500,
      label: {
         text: 'Expected Sales'
      }
   }]
}
```

4. You should have the expected result as shown in the following chart:

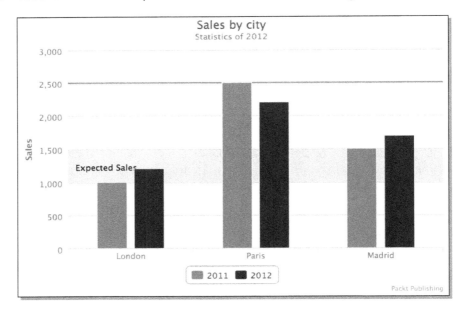

Step 5 – setting the tool tip

The tool tip element appears when you are pointing your mouse over an element. Highcharts sets a default tool tip, but you can override it by setting a new template. In our example, we will modify the tool tip by adding a measurement unit, which will simply be Units in our case.

1. Add the tooltip section and set the parameter valueSuffix with the value Units. This parameter defines the text that will be added at the end of the number.

    ```
    tooltip: {
        valueSuffix: 'Units'
    }
    ```

2. You should have the expected result as shown in the following chart:

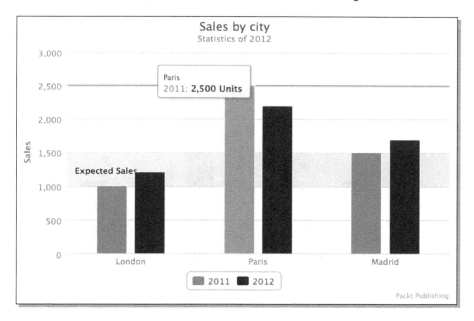

Step 6 – setting the legend

The chart legend can be displayed by default on some Highcharts' charts. Nevertheless, you can hide or customize the legend. In order to retrieve some space in our chart, we will change the legend position to the top right side of the chart.

1. Add the `legend` section. Set the `align` parameter to the right and `verticalAlign` to the top, in order to move the legend to the top right side. Then, set the `floating` parameter to `true`. This parameter will be used in order to have the legend over our chart.

```
legend: {
    align: 'right',
    verticalAlign: 'top',
    floating: true
}
```

2. You should have the expected result as shown in the following chart:

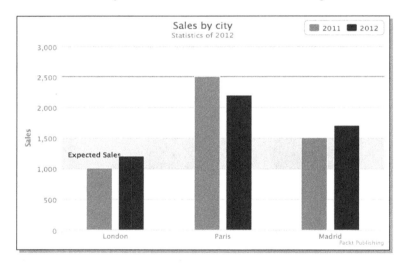

Step 7 – final code

The final code looks like:

```
$(function () {
    var chart = $('#myFirstChartContainer').highcharts({
        chart: {
            type: 'column'
        },
        title: {
            text: 'Sales by city'
        },
        subtitle: {
```

```
                text: 'Statistics of 2012'
            },
            credits: {
                text: 'Packt Publishing',
                href: 'http://www.packtpub.com'
            },
            xAxis: {
                categories: ['London', 'Paris', 'Madrid']
            },
            yAxis: {
                title: {
                    text: 'Sales'
                },
                plotLines: [{
                    color: '#FF0000',
                    width: 2,
                    value: 2500
                }],
                plotBands: [{
                    color: 'rgba(124,252,0, 0.3)',
                    from: 1000,
                    to: 1500,
                    label: {
                        text: 'Expected Sales'
                    }
                }]
            },
            tooltip: {
                valueSuffix: ' Units'
            },
            legend: {
                align: 'right',
                verticalAlign: 'top',
                floating: true
            },
            series: [{
                name: '2011',
                data: [1000, 2500, 1500]
            },
            {
                name: '2012',
                data: [1200, 2200, 1700]
            }]
        });
    });
```

At the end of this section, you have created the main elements that comprise a chart, and you will now be able to reuse it to any charts that you would want to create.

Top 4 features you need to know about

As you start to use Highcharts, you will realize that there are a wide variety of things that you can do with it. This section will teach you all about the most commonly performed tasks and most commonly used features in Highcharts.

Creating a line chart with a time axis and two Y axes

In this section, we will create a line chart with a time axis and two Y axes. We will also customize the chart by customizing the tool tip and by adding the possibility to zoom inside the chart.

We will now create the code for this chart:

1. You start the creation of your chart by implementing the constructor of your Highcharts' chart:

    ```
    var chart = $('#myFirstChartContainer').highcharts({
    });
    ```

2. We will now set the different sections inside the constructor. We start by the chart section. Since we'll be creating a line chart, we define the `type` element with the value `line`. Then, we implement the zoom feature by setting the `zoomType` element. You can set the value to `x`, `y`, or `xy` depending on which axes you want to be able to zoom. For our chart, we will implement the possibility to zoom on the x-axis:

    ```
    chart: {
        type: 'line',
        zoomType: 'x'
    },
    ```

3. We define the title of our chart:

    ```
    title: {
        text: 'Energy consumption linked to the temperature'
    },
    ```

4. Now, we create the x axis. We set the type to `datetime` because we are using time data, and we remove the `title` by setting the `text` to `null`. You need to set a null value in order to disable the title of the `xAxis`:

    ```
    xAxis: {
        type: 'datetime',
        title: {
            text: null
        }
    },
    ```

5. We then configure the Y axes. As defined, we add two Y axes with the titles `Temperature` and `Electricity consumed (in KWh)`, which we override with a minimum value of `0`. We set the `opposite` parameter to `true` for the second axis in order to have the second y axis on the right side:

```
yAxis: [
    {
        title: {
            text: 'Temperature'
        },
        min:0
    },
    {
        title: {
            text: 'Energy consumed (in KWh)'
        },
        opposite:true,
        min:0
    }
],
```

6. We will now customize the `tooltip` section. We use the `crosshairs` option in order to have a line for our `tooltip` that we will use to follow values of both series. Then, we set the shared value to `true` in order to have values of both series on the same `tooltip`.

```
tooltip: {
    crosshairs: true,
    shared: true
},
```

7. Further, we set the series section. For the datetime axes, you can set your series section by using two different ways. You can use the first way when your data follow a regular time interval and the second way when your data don't necessarily follow a regular time interval. We will use both the ways by setting the two series with two different options. The first series follows a regular interval. For this series, we set the `pointInterval` parameter where we define the data interval in milliseconds. For our chart, we set an interval of one day. We set the `pointStart` parameter with the date of the first value. We then set the data section with our values. The `tooltip` section is set with the `valueSuffix` element, where we define the suffix to be added after the value inside our tool tip. We set our `yAxis` element with the axis we want to associate with our series. Because we want to set this series to the first axis, we set the value to `0` (zero). For the second series, we will use the second way because our data is not necessarily following the regular intervals. But you can also use this way, even if your data follows a regular interval. We set our data by couple, where the first element represents the date

and the second element represents the value. We also override the `tooltip` section of the second series. We then set the `yAxis` element with the value 1 because we want to associate this series to the second axis. For your chart, you can also set your date values with a timestamp value instead of using the JavaScript function `Date.UTC`.

```
series: [
    {
        name: 'Temperature',
        pointInterval: 24 * 3600 * 1000,
        pointStart: Date.UTC(2013, 0, 01),
        data: [17.5, 16.2, 16.1, 16.1, 15.9, 15.8, 16.2],
        tooltip: {
            valueSuffix: ' °C'
        },
        yAxis: 0
    },
    {
        name: 'Electricity consumption',
        data: [
            [Date.UTC(2013, 0, 01), 8.1],
            [Date.UTC(2013, 0, 02), 6.2],
            [Date.UTC(2013, 0, 03), 7.3],
            [Date.UTC(2013, 0, 05), 7.1],
            [Date.UTC(2013, 0, 06), 12.3],
            [Date.UTC(2013, 0, 07), 10.2]
        ],
        tooltip: {
            valueSuffix: ' KWh'
        },
        yAxis: 1
    }
]
```

8. You should have this as the final code:

```
$(function () {
    var chart = $('#myFirstChartContainer').highcharts({
        chart: {
            type: 'line',
            zoomType: 'x'
        },
        title: {
            text: 'Energy consumption linked to the temperature'
        },
        xAxis: {
            type: 'datetime',
            title: {
                text: null
            }
        },
        yAxis: [
```

```
            {
                title: {
                    text: 'Temperature'
                },
                min:0
            },
            {
                title: {
                    text: 'Electricity consumed'
                },
                opposite:true,
                min:0
            }
        ],
        tooltip: {
            crosshairs: true,
            shared: true
        },
        series: [
            {
                name: 'Temperature',
                pointInterval: 24 * 3600 * 1000,
                pointStart: Date.UTC(2013, 0, 01),
                data: [17.5, 16.2, 16.1, 16.1, 15.9, 15.8, 16.2],
                tooltip: {
                    valueSuffix: ' °C'
                },
                yAxis: 0
            },
            {
                name: 'Electricity consumption',
                data: [
                    [Date.UTC(2013, 0, 01), 8.1],
                    [Date.UTC(2013, 0, 02), 6.2],
                    [Date.UTC(2013, 0, 03), 7.3],
                    [Date.UTC(2013, 0, 05), 7.1],
                    [Date.UTC(2013, 0, 06), 12.3],
                    [Date.UTC(2013, 0, 07), 10.2]
                ],
                tooltip: {
                    valueSuffix: ' KWh'
                },
                yAxis: 1
            }
        ]
    });
});
```

9. You should have the expected result as shown in the following screenshot:

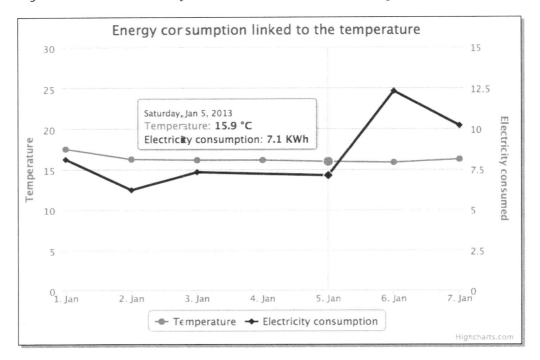

Creating a stacked bar chart

In this section, we will create a stacked bar chart, where we will define the color of the different series.

We will now create the code for this chart:

1. You start the creation of your chart by implementing the constructor of your Highcharts' chart:

```
var chart = $('#myFirstChartContainer').highcharts({
});
```

2. We now set the different sections inside the constructor. We start by the `chart` section. Because we are creating a bar chart, we define the `type` element with the value `bar`:

```
chart: {
    type: 'bar'
},
```

3. We define the title of our chart:

```
title: {
    text: 'Age pyramid of employees'
},
```

4. We create the `xAxis` section. In this section, we set the three categories of our chart:

```
xAxis: {
    categories: ['40-55', '25-40', '18-25']
},
```

5. We configure the `yAxis` section. We set the title of this axis with the value `Number of employees`:

```
yAxis: {
    title: {
        text: 'Number of employees'
    }
},
```

6. We now set the `plotOptions` section. Inside this section, you will be able to customize some parameters for your chart or for your series. For our chart, we customize the `series` element by setting the stacking option to `normal`. You can also set this value to `percent`, if you prefer to stack by using percentages instead of values.

```
plotOptions: {
    series: {
        stacking: 'normal'
    }
},
```

7. Further, we configure the series section of our chart. We set two series with the name `Male` and `Female` and a set of data. Then, we set the `stack` parameter. The `stack` parameter defines the stacking groups. You can set this value with a number, a string, or other types of data. If you want to stack several series together, your different series will have to match the same value. For our chart, we set this element for our two series with the value `1`. Finally, we define the color of our series by overriding the color element in the hexadecimal format.

```
series: [
    {
        name: 'Male',
        data: [835, 2635, 1437],
        stack: 1,
        color: '#6495ED'
    },
    {
        name: 'Female',
```

```
        data: [785, 2435, 1657],
        stack: 1,
        color: '#DC143C'
    }
]
```

8. You should have the expected code as follows:

```
$(function () {
    var chart = $('#myFirstChartContainer').highcharts({
        chart: {
            type: 'bar'
        },
        title: {
            text: 'Age pyramid of employees'
        },
        xAxis: {
            categories: ['40-55', '25-40', '18-25']
        },
        yAxis: {
            title: {
                text: 'Number of employees'
            }
        },
        plotOptions: {
            series: {
                stacking: 'normal'
            }
        },
        series: [
            {
                name: 'Male',
                data: [835, 2635, 1437],
                stack: 1,
                color: '#6495ED'
            },
            {
                name: 'Female',
                data: [785, 2435, 1657],
                stack: 1,
                color: '#DC143C'
            }
        ]
    });
});
```

9. You should have the expected result:

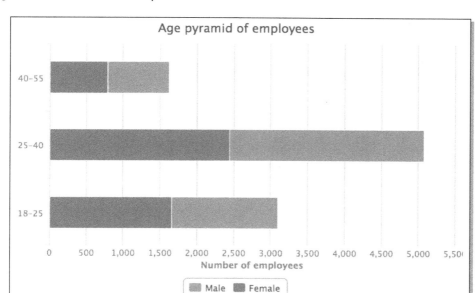

Creating a pie chart

In this section, we will create a pie chart. Compared to charts that we have created in the previous section, this type of chart doesn't contain any axes.

We will now create the code of this chart:

1. You start the creation of your chart by implementing the constructor of your Highcharts' chart:

```
var chart = $('#myFirstChartContainer').highcharts({
});
```

2. We now set the different sections inside the constructor. We start with the `chart` section. Since we are creating a pie chart, we define the `type` element with the value `pie`:

```
chart: {
    type: 'pie'
},
```

3. We define the title of our chart:

```
title: {
    text: 'Operating Systems used in a company'
},
```

4. We customize the display of the chart by overriding the plotOptions section. Because we are creating a pie chart, we override the parameters of the subsection pie. We set the allowPointSelect attribute to true in order to have an interactive chart when a user clicks on some part of the pie chart. For the pie chart, the legend is not displayed by default. In order to display the legend, we set the showInLegend attribute to true. Then, we override the tooltip section in order to add the percentage suffix inside our tool tip. Finally, we create labels around the chart by implementing the dataLabels attribute. Inside this attribute, we set enabled to true in order to activate this feature. Then, the color attribute defines the color of the label and the connectorColor attribute defines the color of the line between the pie chart and the label. The formatter option defines a function that is used in order to format our label. When you implement the formatter parameter for any type of chart, you can use the following data for your template:

   ○ this.percentage: It is the percentage of your selection (For stacked and pie charts only).

   ○ this.point: It is the point object. You can access to some information of the point object, such as the point name with this.point name. If you use a JavaScript debugger, such as Firebug, you will be able to know all data available for this object.

   ○ this.series: It is the series object. You can access to some information concerning the selected series, such as the series name with this.series.name. If you use a JavaScript debugger, such as Firebug, you will be able to know all data available for this object.

   ○ this.total: It is the total of all your values for stacked series only.

   ○ this.x: It is the x value.

   ○ this.y: It is the y value.

5. For our chart, the label will display the point name in bold with the percentage of the data

```
plotOptions: {
    pie: {
        allowPointSelect: true,
        showInLegend: true,
        tooltip: {
            valueSuffix: ' %'
        },
        dataLabels: {
            enabled: true,
            color: '#000000',
            connectorColor: '#888888',
            formatter: function() {
                return '<b>'+ this.point.name +'</b>: '+
```

```
            this.percentage +' %';
        }
    }
}
},
```

6. We then set the `series` section. For pie charts, you only need to create one series with a `name` and your `data`. You can set your data in two different ways. The first way consists of using couple of data, with the name of your element in the first parameter and your value in the second parameter. The second way consists of using an array of objects with several attributes, such as `name` which defines the name of the object, `color` which defines the color your data, and `y` which defines the data value. The second way can be used when you want to manually set the color of your data. For our series, we will use both ways, but for your own chart, you may choose the best option for your project.

```
series: [{
    name: 'Operating Systems',
    data: [
        ['Windows 7', 45],
        ['Windows XP', 35], //First way
        {
          name: 'Mac OS X',
          color: '#CC0033','
          y: 20
        } //Second way
    ]
}]
```

7. You should get the following code:

```
$(function () {
    var chart = $('#myFirstChartContainer').highcharts({
        chart: {
            type: 'pie'
        },
        title: {
            text: 'Operating Systems used in a company'
        },
        plotOptions: {
            pie: {
                allowPointSelect: true,
                showInLegend: true,
                tooltip: {
                    valueSuffix: ' %'
                },
                dataLabels: {
                    enabled: true,
```

```
                    color: '#000000',
                    connectorColor: '#888888',
                    formatter: function() {
                        return '<b>'+ this.point.name +'</b>: '+
                                this.percentage +' %';
                    }
                }
            }
        },
        series: [{
            name: 'Operating Systems',
            data: [
                ['Windows 7', 45],
                ['Windows XP', 35], //First way
                {
                    name: 'Mac OS X',
                    color: '#CC0033',
                    y  20
                } //Second way
            ]
        }]
    });
});
```

8. You should have the expected result as follows:

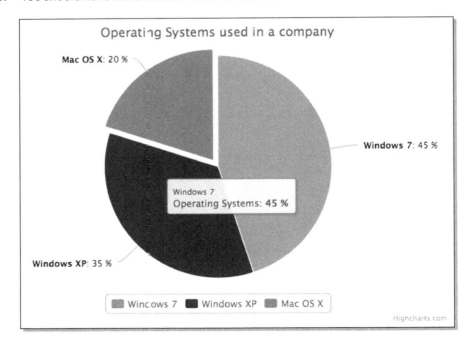

Creating dynamic charts

In the previous sections, we have created static charts. In this section, we will create a dynamic area chart by using Ajax technology. Highcharts charts are set with the **JavaScript Object Notation (JSON)** notation, which is used in JavaScript in order to represent objects by using couple of attributes and values, such as in the following code:

```
{
    attribute1: "value1",
    attribute2: 2,
    attributeArray: [0,1,2],
    subcategory:
    {
        attribute3: "value3"
    }
}
```

For the creation of our dynamic chart, we will firstly create our JSON string on the server side. For our example we will use PHP language, but you can use any programming language. Then, this JSON string will be retrieved on the client side by sending an Ajax request, and will be converted into a JSON object. This JSON object will be reused inside our Highcharts constructor.

We begin by creating our server side script `server_side.php`. You can create your JSON string directly by using your programming language or use some libraries, such as `json_encode` for PHP or JSON library in Java. In our case, we will use the `json_encode` function, which transforms associative arrays into JSON objects. In order to have a more readable code, we will create PHP variables for each section of our Highcharts' chart, which we will gather into a single array. Then, this array will be encoded into a JSON string at the end of our script.

1. We start our JSON string by creating the chart section. Because we are creating an area chart, we create an associative array with the key `type` and the value `area`:

   ```
   $chartSection = array('type' => 'area');
   ```

2. We set the title section of our chart. We create an associative array with the key `text` and the value `Sales evolution`:

   ```
   $titleSection = array('text' => 'Sales evolution');
   ```

3. We set the category section of our chart. We create an associative array with the key `categories` and the value with an array of categories:

   ```
   $xAxisSection = array('categories' => array('Jan', 'Feb', 'Mar', 'Apr'));
   ```

4. We set the `yAxisSection` of our chart. We create an associative array with the key `title` and the value with another associative array with a key `text` and a value `Sales`:

```
$yAxisSection = array('title' => array('text' => 'Sales'));
```

5. We set the `seriesSection` of our chart. We create an array with an associative array with the key `name` and a value `Cities` and the key `data` and an array of data as values:

```
$seriesSection = array(array('name' => 'Cities', 'data' =>
array(1250, 1500, 1300, 1450)))
```

6. We regroup all our variables already created inside an associative array with the keys `chart`, `title`, `xAxis`, `yAxis` and `series`, which correspond to our main Highcharts sections:

```
$highchartChart = array('chart' => $chartSection, 'title' =>
$titleSection, 'xAxis' => $xAxisSection, 'yAxis' => $yAxisSection,
'series' => $seriesSection);
```

7. We transform our final array into a JSON string by using the function `json_encode`, which will be displayed in output:

```
echo json_encode($highchartChart);
```

8. You should have the following code:

```php
<?php
    $chartSection = array('type' => 'area');

    $titleSection = array('text' => 'Sales evolution');

    $xAxisSection = array('categories' => array('Jan',
      'Feb','Mar', 'Apr'));

    $yAxisSection = array('title' => array('text' =>
      'Sales'));

    $seriesSection = array(array('name' => 'Sales', 'data'
      => array(1250, 1500, 1300, 1450)));

    $highchartChart = array('chart' => $chartSection,'title'
      => $titleSection, 'xAxis' => $xAxisSection, 'yAxis' =>
        $yAxisSection, 'series' => $seriesSection);

    echo json_encode($highchartChart);
?>
```

9. You should obtain the following output. It has been formatted to make it more readable.

```
{
        "chart":{
                "type":"area"
        },
        "title":{
                "text":"Sales evolution"
        },
        "xAxis":{
                "categories":["Jan","Feb","Mar","Apr"]
        },
        "yAxis":{
                "title":{
                        "text":"Sales"
                }
        },
        "series":[
                {
                        "name":"Sales",
                        "data":[1250,1500,1300,1450]
                }
        ]
}
```

You can also create your JSON string with your own logic and with your own data retrieved within a database or other data sources.

Now that we have created our JSON string, we will create our script on the client side:

1. We start the creation of our script by creating the Ajax request. We use the `ajax` function of jQuery with the URL of our server side script in parameter. We override the `success` function in order to retrieve the result of our `ajax` request.

   ```
   $.ajax("http://localhost:8080/server_side.php", {
      success: function (result) {
      }
   });
   ```

2. Inside the `success` function, we transform our JSON string into a `json object`:

   ```
   var jsonObject = jQuery.parseJSON(result);
   ```

3. Then, we create our Highcharts' chart by using our `jsonObject` inside our constructor:

   ```
   var chart = $('#myFirstChartContainer').highcharts(jsonObject);
   ```

4. You should have the following code on the client side:

```
$(function () {
    $.ajax("http://localhost:8080/server_side.php", {
        success: function (result) {
          var jsonObject = jQuery.parseJSON(result)
          var chart =
$('#myFirstChartContainer').highcharts(jsonObject);
          }
    });

});
```

5. You should have the following result:

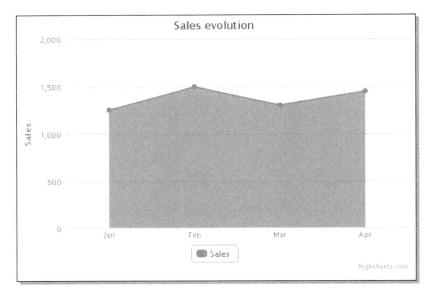

People and places you should get to know

If you need help with Highcharts, this section will be an invaluable reference.

Official sites

✦ Highcharts homepage: `http://www.highcharts.com`

✦ General documentation: `http://docs.highcharts.com`

✦ Demo: `http://www.highcharts.com/demo/`

✦ API documentation: `http://api.highcharts.com/highcharts`

JSFiddle tool

When you will start to explore the Highcharts API documentation, you will find several links that will allow you to try some parts of Highcharts' API by using the JSFiddle tool (`http://jsfiddle.net`). These links will allow you to discover the meanings of each parameter in order to choose whether you want to implement it in your chart.

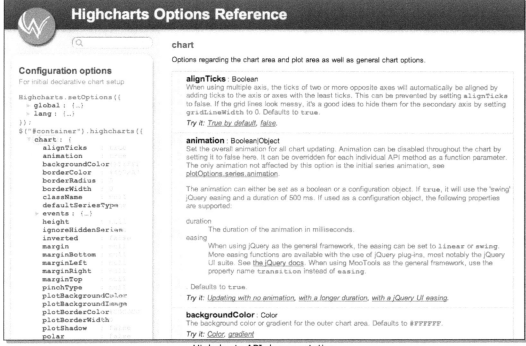

Highcharts API documentation

When you click on these links, you will be redirected to the JSFiddle website with some example code loaded. With this online tool, you will be able to modify some parameters of your chart for testing, and to see the results directly in your browser by clicking on the **Run** button.

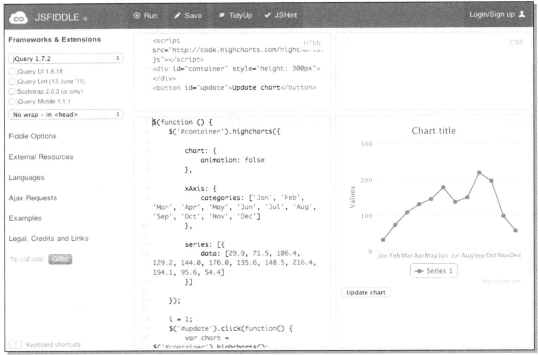

JSFiddle online tool

By exploring these different links, and by trying yourself to modify a few options of Highcharts, you will be able to customize your chart according to your needs.

Articles and tutorials

Some screencasts display how to use Highcharts with the jQuery library, as well as other ways to create your chart with your data: http://www.youtube.com/playlist?list=PLUpnKy5Si8zB CzuNydm4FUEHtwEQkgUqR.

Community

+ Official mailing list: `http://www.highcharts.com/download` (At the bottom of the page)

+ Official forums: `http://highslide.com/forum/`

+ Support: `http://www.highcharts.com/support`

+ User FAQ: `http://docs.highcharts.com/#faq`

Blogs

The blog of *Joe Kuan*, author of the book *Learning Highcharts, Packt Publishing* can be found at `http://joekuan.wordpress.com`.

Twitter

+ Follow Highcharts on Twitter: `https://twitter.com/Highcharts`

+ For more Open Source information, follow Packt at `http://twitter.com/#!/packtopensource`.

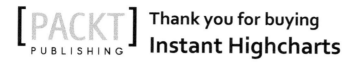

Thank you for buying
Instant Highcharts

About Packt Publishing

Packt, pronounced 'packed', published its first book "*Mastering phpMyAdmin for Effective MySQL Management*" in April 2004 and subsequently continued to specialize in publishing highly focused books on specific technologies and solutions.

Our books and publications share the experiences of your fellow IT professionals in adapting and customizing today's systems, applications, and frameworks. Our solution based books give you the knowledge and power to customize the software and technologies you're using to get the job done. Packt books are more specific and less general than the IT books you have seen in the past. Our unique business model allows us to bring you more focused information, giving you more of what you need to know, and less of what you don't.

Packt is a modern, yet unique publishing company, which focuses on producing quality, cutting-edge books for communities of developers, administrators, and newbies alike. For more information, please visit our website: www.packtpub.com.

Writing for Packt

We welcome all inquiries from people who are interested in authoring. Book proposals should be sent to author@packtpub.com. If your book idea is still at an early stage and you would like to discuss it first before writing a formal book proposal, contact us; one of our commissioning editors will get in touch with you.

We're not just looking for published authors; if you have strong technical skills but no writing experience, our experienced editors can help you develop a writing career, or simply get some additional reward for your expertise.

Vaadin 7 Cookbook

ISBN: 978-1-84951-880-2   Paperback: 404 pages

Over 90 recipes for creating Rich Internet Applications with the latest version of Vaadin

1. Covers exciting features such as using drag and n anddrop, creating charts, custom components, lazy loading, server-push functionality, and more

2. Tips for facilitating the development and testing of Vaadin applications

3. Enhance your applications with Spring, Grails, or Roo integration

Learning Highcharts

ISBN: 978-1-84951-908-3   Paperback: 362 pages

Create rich, intuitive, and interactive JavaScript data visualization for your web and enterprise development needs using this powerful charting library — Highcharts

1. Step-by-step instructions with real-live data to create bar charts, column charts and pie charts, to easily create artistic and professional quality charts

2. Learn tips and tricks to create a variety of charts such as horizontal gauge charts, projection charts, and circular ratio charts

3. Use and integrate Highcharts with jQuery Mobile and ExtJS 4, and understand how to run Highcharts on the server-side

Please check **www.PacktPub.com** for information on our titles

Data Visualization: a successful design process

ISBN: 978-1-84969-346-2   Paperback: 206 pages

A structured design approach to equip you with the knowledge of how to successfully accomplish any data visualization challenge efficiently and effectively

1. A portable, versatile and flexible data visualization design approach that will help you navigate the complex path towards success

2. Explains the many different reasons for creating visualizations and identifies the key parameters which lead to very different design options

3. Thorough explanation of the many visual variables and visualization taxonomy to provide you with a menu of creative options

Google Visualization API Essentials

ISBN: 978-1-84969-436-0   Paperback: 252 pages

Make sense of your data: make it visual with the Google Visualization API

1. Wrangle all sorts of data into a visual format, without being an expert programmer

2. Visualize new or existing spreadsheet data through charts, graphs, and maps

3. Full of diagrams, core concept explanations, best practice tips, and links to working book examples

Please check **www.PacktPub.com** for information on our titles

www.ingramcontent.com/pod-product-compliance
Lightning Source LLC
LaVergne TN
LVHW080119070326
832902LV00015B/2673